To Jim, Rita, Colin & CHELSEA,

HAPPY NEW YEAR (2004)

& Much Love,

Mark & Paula

MARY BAKER EDDY:
"UNDER THE SHADOW OF THE ALMIGHTY"

FOREWORD

The purpose of this book is to acquaint the reader with the life and mission of Mary Baker Eddy, the Discoverer and Founder of Christian Science. Unlike other biographies of Mrs. Eddy, it allows her life-story to unfold not through the words of a single writer, but through selected quotations from Mrs. Eddy's own writings, from those who knew her, from other writers of her day, and from the Scriptures.

Mary Baker Eddy: "Under the Shadow of the Almighty" includes chapters about Mrs. Eddy's childhood, the Bible and its influence on her discovery, and her role as author, healer, and Leader of the Christian Science movement. It also contains original artwork depicting certain events in Mrs. Eddy's life, historical photographs pertinent to the subject matter, and photographs of biblical sites.

The book was compiled with young people in mind, but it may be enjoyed by anyone, regardless of age. Parents, when working with children, may want to familiarize themselves first with the book's quotations and then utilize the "Sources for Quotations" pages in the back of the book. This will give parents the context surrounding each reference. Questions are also provided at the end of every section to help the parent and child review the material. Parents and children might look together at the list of historical events taking place throughout Mrs. Eddy's lifetime, noting the acceleration of development on the human scene subsequent to her discovery of Christian Science.

It is hoped that this book will foster an appreciation for the uniqueness of Mary Baker Eddy's life and encourage the reader to gain a deeper sense of her life-purpose, as she defines it: "...to impress humanity with the genuine recognition of practical, operative Christian Science" (*Miscellaneous Writings* 207:4).

MARY BAKER EDDY:
"UNDER THE SHADOW OF THE ALMIGHTY"

Salt Sea, Israel

MARY BAKER EDDY:
"UNDER THE SHADOW OF THE ALMIGHTY"

Compiler: Kristy L. Christian
Original illustrations: Robin Orbach Starke

Infinite Discovery, Inc.
Oklahoma City, Oklahoma

MARY BAKER EDDY:
"UNDER THE SHADOW OF THE ALMIGHTY"

by Kristy L. Christian and Robin Orbach Starke

Title taken from Ps. 91:1

Printed in the United States of America
Publisher's Cataloging-in-Publication
(provided by Infinite Discovery, Inc., Oklahoma City, OK)

Preassigned LCCN: 2001-135717

ISBN: 0-9626535-4-3

All Bible quotations are taken from the King James Version unless otherwise noted.

MARY BAKER EDDY:
"UNDER THE SHADOW OF THE ALMIGHTY"

ACKNOWLEDGMENTS

We are indebted to those early workers in Christian Science
who knew Mary Baker Eddy and recorded their reminiscences...

to those biographers of Mary Baker Eddy who researched to
share with the world statements by Mrs. Eddy...

to those Christian Science practitioners and teachers whose dedication
to the Cause of Christian Science and love of its Discoverer and Founder, Mary Baker Eddy,
have made an indelible impact on the world through their healing work...

to parents, Sunday School teachers, and others
who have taught the children to love Mary Baker Eddy...

and special thanks
to Carolee M. Watt
who urged that this book be written in order
for children and adults to learn more about
Mary Baker Eddy.

K.L.C.
R.O.S.

MARY BAKER EDDY:
"UNDER THE SHADOW OF THE ALMIGHTY"

For permission to reproduce copyrighted or other material, grateful acknowledgment is made to the following:

Scala/Art Resource, New York City, New York

New Hampshire Historical Society, Concord, New Hampshire

Daystar Foundation and Library, Oklahoma City, Oklahoma

Photographs on page 91 courtesy of Longyear Museum, Chestnut Hill, Massachusetts

CONTENTS

"Mere historic incidents and personal events are frivolous and of no moment, unless they illustrate the ethics of Truth."

Mary Baker Eddy

1821 July 16 — Mary Morse Baker born in Bow, New Hampshire.

1838 July 26 — Joins Congregational Church at Sanbornton Bridge (Tilton), New Hampshire.

1843 December 10 — Marries George Washington Glover; sails for Charleston, South Carolina (December 25).

1844 June 27 — George Washington Glover dies; Mrs. Glover returns home to New Hampshire three weeks later.

September 12 — Gives birth to George Washington Glover II.

1853 June 21 — Marries Dr. Daniel Patterson.

1866 February 1 — Falls on ice in Lynn, Massachusetts; three days later is healed of injury.

1872 February — Begins writing *Science and Health*.

1873 November — Divorces Dr. Patterson (whose name she had discontinued using in 1866).

1875 March — Mary Baker Glover buys No. 8 Broad Street, Lynn, Massachusetts; writes final pages of *Science and Health* in her attic room.

October 30 — First edition of *Science and Health* published.

1877 January 1 — Mary Baker Glover marries Asa Gilbert Eddy.

1879 April 12 — Christian Science Church founded.

1881 Massachusetts Metaphysical College chartered.

First Christian Science Sunday School conducted by Asa Gilbert Eddy, superintendent.

1882 June 2 Asa Gilbert Eddy dies.

1883 April 14 First issue of the *Journal of Christian Science* published (renamed *The Christian Science Journal* in 1885).

1888 Opens the first Christian Science Reading Room.

1889 December "The Christian Science Bible Lessons" issued (forerunner of *The Christian Science Quarterly*, first published in April of 1890). Formally disorganized the Church.

1892 June 20 Mrs. Eddy moves to "Pleasant View" home in Concord, New Hampshire.

September 23 The First Church of Christ, Scientist, organized with 12 members.

1894 December 19 Ordains Bible and *Science and Health* as pastor of The Mother Church.

December 30 First church service held in the Original Edifice of The Mother Church.

1895 January 6 Dedicatory service held in The Mother Church.

1898 January Christian Science Board of Lectureship established.

July *The Christian Science Quarterly* with 26 lesson subjects initiated.

September 1 First issue of *The Christian Science Weekly* published (renamed *Christian Science Sentinel* in January 1899).

IMPORTANT DATES IN
MARY BAKER EDDY'S LIFE

1899 July 31 — Libel suit filed against Mrs. Eddy by Josephine Curtis Woodbury.

1901 June 5 — Mrs. Woodbury's suit is lost.

1906 June 10 — The Mother Church Extension dedicated.

1907 March 1 — "Next friends" suit filed by Mrs. Eddy's son, George W. Glover, his daughter, Mary Baker Glover, and his cousin George W. Baker.

August 21 — Petition of "next friends" withdrawn.

1908 January 26 — Mrs. Eddy leaves "Pleasant View" in Concord, New Hampshire, and moves into Chestnut Hill home near Boston.

November 25 — First issue of *The Christian Science Monitor* published.

1910 December 3 — Mrs. Eddy (in her 90th year) passes on at her Chestnut Hill home.

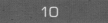

1875 — *Science and Health* (first edition) (*Key to the Scriptures* added to title in 1883; in 1881 the cross-and-crown seal added to the third edition)

1876 — *The Science of Man, By Which the Sick Are Healed, Embracing Questions and Answers in Moral Science* (becomes part of the chapter "Recapitulation" in *Science and Health* in 1881)

1880 — *Christian Healing*

1883 — *The People's Idea of God: Its Effect on Health and Christianity*

1885 — *Historical Sketch of Metaphysical Healing* (revised in 1891 under title *Retrospection and Introspection*)

1885 — *Defence of Christian Science* (published as *Christian Science: No and Yes* in 1887)

1887 — *Rudiments and Rules of Divine Science* (renamed *Rudimental Divine Science* in 1891)

1888 — *Unity of Good and Unreality of Evil* (renamed *Unity of Good* in 1891)

1893 — *Christ and Christmas* (withdrawn 1894; republished in December 1897)

1895 — *Pulpit and Press*

1895 — *Manual of The Mother Church* (first edition)

PUBLISHED WRITINGS OF
MARY BAKER EDDY

1897 — *Miscellaneous Writings*

1898 — *Christian Science* versus *Pantheism*

1900 — *Message to The Mother Church for 1900*

1901 — *Message to The Mother Church for 1901*

1902 — *Message to The Mother Church for 1902*

1910 — *Poetical Works*

1913 — *The First Church of Christ, Scientist, and Miscellany*

❖

1903 — *Concordance to Science and Health with Key to the Scriptures,* Albert F. Conant, Compiler

1915 — *A Complete Concordance to the Writings of Mary Baker Eddy other than Science and Health with Key to the Scriptures*

Dedicated to the Childlike Thought:

"**W**illingness to become as a little child and
to leave the old for the new, renders thought
receptive of the advanced idea."

Mary Baker Eddy

"**C**HILDREN.
The spiritual thoughts
and representatives
of Life, Truth, and Love."

Mary Baker Eddy

"**S**ee what love the Father has given us,
that we should be called children
of God; and that is what we are."

I John

"Beloved children, the world has need of you,
— and more as children than as men and women:
it needs your innocence, unselfishness, faithful affection,
uncontaminated lives. You need also to watch, and pray that
you preserve these virtues unstained, and lose them not
through contact with the world. What grander ambition
is there than to maintain in yourselves what Jesus loved,
and to know that your example, more than words,
makes morals for mankind!"

Mary Baker Eddy

"Train up a child in the way he should go:
and when he is old, he will not depart from it."

Proverbs

"...narrow is the way..." The Gospel of Matthew

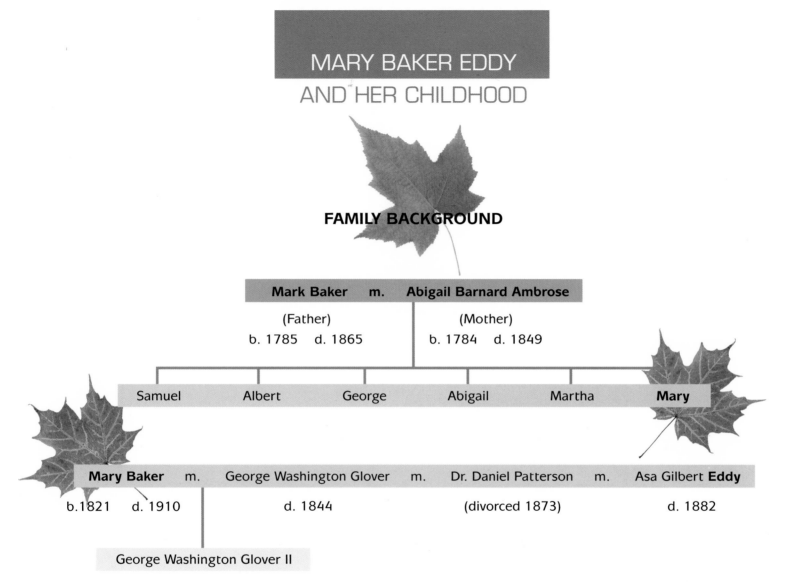

MARY BAKER EDDY
AND HER CHILDHOOD

FAMILY BACKGROUND

Mark Baker   m.   **Abigail Barnard Ambrose**

(Father)   (Mother)

b. 1785   d. 1865   b. 1784   d. 1849

Samuel	Albert	George	Abigail	Martha	**Mary**

Mary Baker   m.   George Washington Glover   m.   Dr. Daniel Patterson   m.   Asa Gilbert **Eddy**

b.1821   d. 1910   d. 1844   (divorced 1873)   d. 1882

George Washington Glover II

b. 1844   d. 1915

A description of Abigail Baker, Mary's mother:

"As a mother, she was untiring in her efforts to secure the happiness of her family.... Her life was a living illustration of Christian faith."

Rev. Richard S. Rust

"...before thou camest forth out
of the womb I sanctified thee,
and I ordained thee a prophet
unto the nations."

Jeremiah

Abigail Baker, when carrying baby Mary,
told her close friend Sally Gault that she had
"a unique conviction about the child....
she could not keep herself from the
conviction that the expected child
was set apart by God."

Jewel Spangler Smaus

Mary Baker was born in Bow, New Hampshire, July 16, 1821.

Courtesy of New Hampshire Historical Society

Photo by M. French, March 3, 1899

Childhood home of Mary Baker

MARY BAKER EDDY
AND HER CHILDHOOD

"...one old apple-tree
bloomed each
spring at the
chamber window
where Mary Baker
first saw the light...."

Sibyl Wilbur

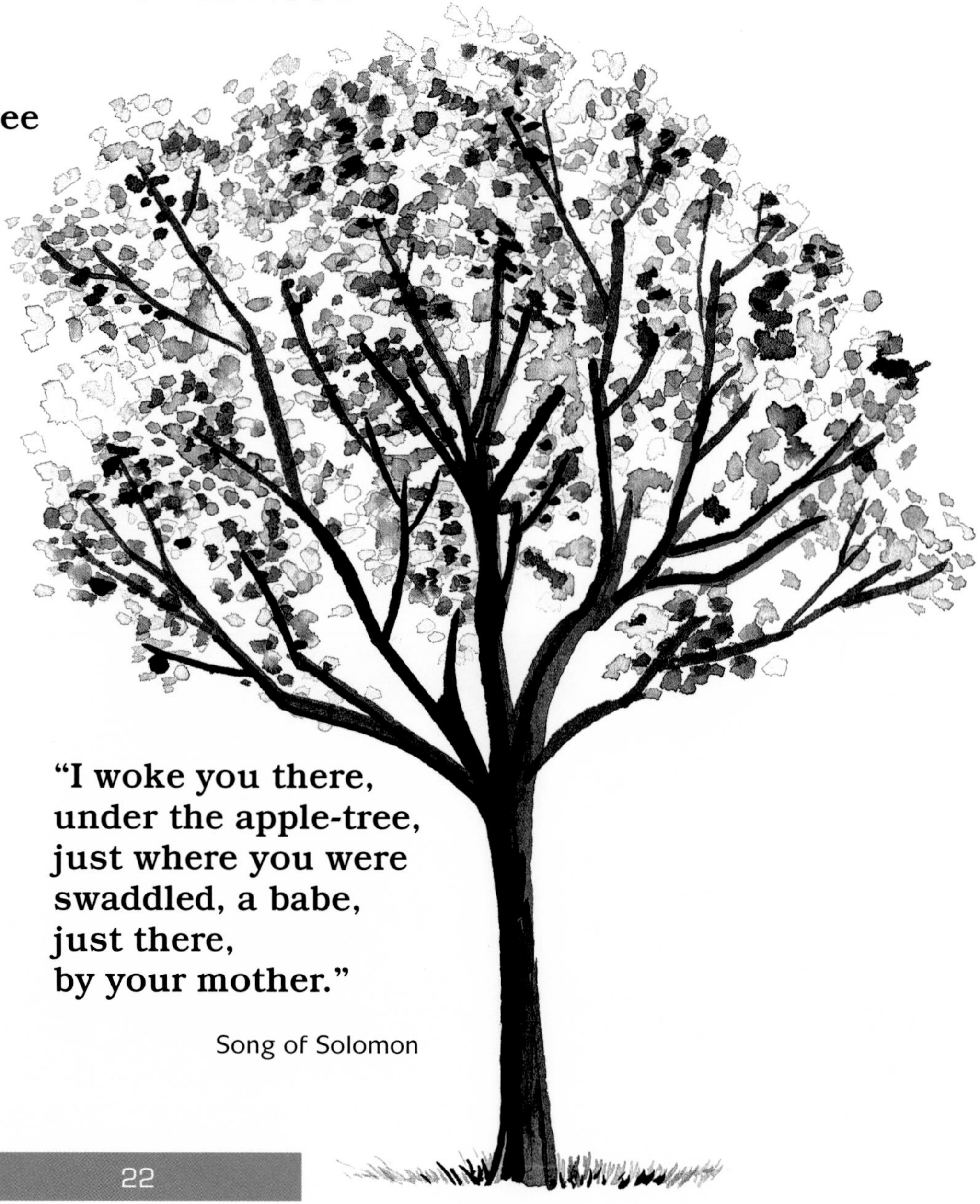

"I woke you there,
under the apple-tree,
just where you were
swaddled, a babe,
just there,
by your mother."

Song of Solomon

"The tradition still lingers in Bow that when the children were playing together Mary would every now and then slip away and be found later on top of a great rock, reading." Robert Peel

Courtesy of Daystar Foundation and Library, Jewel Spangler Smaus collection

Bow, New Hampshire

"In and out
of season Mary was
always the champion of the
weak and oppressed. In the
school at Bow there was an older
girl who played the tyrant over the
smaller children and was such a
young terror that even the boys
feared her....Mary resolved to do
something about it."

Irving C. Tomlinson

"I could not have been more than eight years of age, but I planted myself in the aisle down which she was coming and exclaimed, 'You shall not touch one of them. I will not permit it'....The teacher confessed to me that I had done what whipping had failed to do, for I had completely changed her character."

Mary Baker Eddy

12

At the age of 12 years at a revival meeting in Concord, New Hampshire, Mary made a profession of faith and spoke of her pure devotion to God.

"...[Rev. Enoch Corser] considered [Mary], even at an early age, superior both intellectually and spiritually to any other woman in Tilton [then Sanbornton Bridge]...."

Bartlett Corser

Courtesy of New Hampshire Historical Society

Rev. Enoch Corser is thought to be the clergyman who received Mary into the Congregational Church.

"My father's relentless theology emphasized belief in a final judgment-day, in the danger of endless punishment, and in a Jehovah merciless towards unbelievers.... My mother, as she bathed my burning temples, bade me lean on God's love....I prayed....The fever was gone....the 'horrible decree' of predestination... forever lost its power over me."

Mary Baker Eddy

Mary Baker Eddy writes in her autobiography about her interview with the pastor of the Congregational Church:

"...I was ready for his doleful questions, which I answered without a tremor, declaring that never could I unite with the church, if assent to this doctrine [of predestination] was essential.... I stoutly maintained that I was willing to trust God, and take my chance of spiritual safety... even if my creedal doubts left me outside the doors. The minister then wished me to tell him when I had experienced a change of heart ....I replied that I could only answer him in the words of the Psalmist: 'Search me, O God, and know my heart: try me, and know my thoughts: and see if there be any wicked way in me, and lead me in the way everlasting.' This was so earnestly said, that even the oldest church-members wept....To the astonishment of many, the good clergyman's heart also melted, and he received me into their communion, and my protest along with me."

Mary Baker Eddy

MARY BAKER EDDY
AND HER CHILDHOOD

"...my religious experience seemed to culminate at twelve years of age."

Mary Baker Eddy

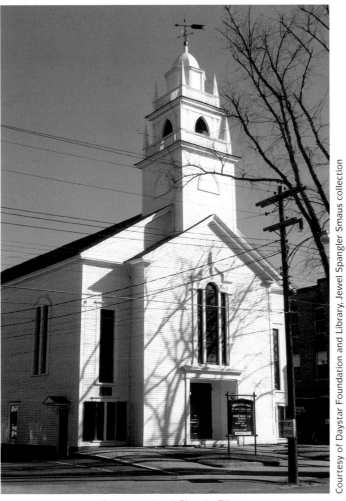

Courtesy of Daystar Foundation and Library, Jewel Spangler Smaus collection

Congregational Church, Tilton
(Sanbornton Bridge), New Hampshire

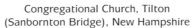

As a child Mary Baker loved to write. She wrote poetry as early as the age of ten.

"...[Mary] announced at a precocious age that when she grew up she would 'write a book.'"

Robert Peel

The following is a poem Mary Baker wrote in childhood.

RESOLUTIONS FOR THE DAY

To rise in the morning and drink in
   the view —
The home where I dwell in the
   vale,
The blossoms whose fragrance
   and charms ever new
Are scattered o'er hillside and
   dale;

To gaze on the sunbeams
   enkindlng the sky —
A loftier life to invite —
A light that illumines my spiritual
   eye,
And inspires my pen as I write;

To form resolutions, with strength
   from on high,
Such physical laws to obey,
As reason with appetite, pleasures
   deny,
That health may my efforts repay;

To kneel at the altar of mercy and
   pray
That pardon and grace, through
   His Son,
May comfort my soul all the
   wearisome day,
   And cheer me with hope when 'tis
   done;

To daily remember my blessings
   and charge,
   And make this my humble
   request:
Increase Thou my faith and my
   vision enlarge,
And bless me with Christ's
   promised rest;

To hourly seek for deliverance
   strong
From selfishness, sinfulness,
   dearth,
From vanity, folly, and all that is
   wrong —
With ambition that binds us to
   earth;

To kindly pass over a wound, or a
   foe
(And mem'ry but part us awhile),
To breathe forth a prayer that His
   love I may know,
Whose mercies my sorrows beguile, —

If these resolutions are acted up to,
   And faith spreads her pinions
   abroad,
'Twill be sweet when I ponder the
   days may be few
That waft me away to my God.

"From my very childhood I was impelled, by a hunger and thirst after divine things...to seek diligently for the knowledge of God as the one great and ever-present relief from human woe."

Mary Baker Eddy

"Blessed are they which do hunger and thirst after righteousness: for they shall be filled."

The Gospel of Matthew

Traditional site of the Mount of Beatitudes
Galilee, Israel

Can you find the answers to these questions?

✍ What are the names of Mary's mother and father?

✍ Can you name Mary's brothers and sisters?

✍ What did Rev. Richard S. Rust write about Mary's mother?

✍ What "unique conviction" did Mary's mother have about her unborn child?

✍ When was Mary born? ✍ Where?

✍ When Mary was eight years old, how did she help her schoolmates?

✍ When Mary was still a little girl, she announced she would do something in her adult years. What was that?

✍ At the age of 12 Mary attended a revival meeting in Concord, New Hampshire. What did Mary Baker object to in her interview with a pastor? ✍ Was she still permitted to join the Congregational church in spite of her protest?

✍ Can you explain the poem Mary wrote? ✍ Which verses indicate her spiritual understanding? ✍ How would you put this poem in your own words?

MARY BAKER EDDY
AND THE BIBLE

"Thy word is a lamp
unto my feet, and a light
unto my path."

Psalms

"Abigail [Mary's mother] read the Bible frequently to the little girl, and the two talked together about the stories of Jesus' healings. Mary felt a special joy in her mother's promise, 'God is able to raise you up from sickness.'...She longed to be so close to God that she could understand all she read in the Bible."

Jewel Spangler Smaus

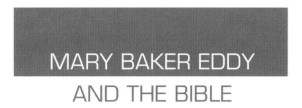

"...in my childhood days,

I would much rather

study the Bible or listen

to a discussion of it

than to go out to play

with the children."

Mary Baker Eddy

"One evening, tucked in bed, when she was only eight years old, Mary listened to a discussion over a Bible text that lasted for a solid three hours. When, many years later, Mrs. Eddy mentioned this incident to her household, someone asked her if she had not grown sleepy. Mrs. Eddy replied in substance: 'Never — I always wanted to know who won.'"

Irving C. Tomlinson

"...the Lord called Samuel: and he answered, Here am I....And the Lord called yet again, Samuel. And Samuel arose and went to Eli, and said, Here am I....And the Lord called Samuel again the third time. And he arose and went to Eli, and said, Here am I; for thou didst call me. And Eli perceived that the Lord had called the child. Therefore Eli said unto Samuel, Go, lie down: and it shall be, if he call thee, that thou shalt say, Speak, Lord; for thy servant heareth....And the Lord came, and stood, and called as at other times, Samuel, Samuel. Then Samuel answered, Speak; for thy servant heareth."

I Samuel

"...when I was about eight years old, I repeatedly heard a voice, calling me distinctly by name, three times....I thought this was my mother's voice, and sometimes went to her, beseeching her to tell me what she wanted. Her answer was always, 'Nothing, child!'....One day, when my cousin, Mehitable Huntoon, was visiting us...the call came again, so loud that Mehitable heard it....That night, before going to rest, my mother read to me the Scriptural narrative of little Samuel, and bade me, when the voice called again, to reply as he did, 'Speak, Lord; for Thy servant heareth.'...When the call came again I did answer, in the words of Samuel...."

Mary Baker Eddy

"Now when Daniel knew that the writing was signed,
he went into his house; and his windows being open
in his chamber toward Jerusalem, he kneeled upon
his knees three times a day, and prayed,
and gave thanks before his God...."

Daniel

"At the age of not more than eight years one of her favorite Bible stories was of Daniel and how with 'his window open in his chamber toward Jerusalem, he kneeled three times a day, and prayed, and gave thanks before his God.' Emulating Daniel, the little girl left the house, went into the woodshed where she could be alone, and there prayed not three times daily but seven times."

Norman Beasley

Temple Mount, Jerusalem, Israel

"After school I would seat myself in the rocker, and while I rocked read the Psalms of David or the life of the Master. At twelve years of age my dear Book of books was well thumbed and worn, and many of my favorite Psalms and whole chapters of the New Testament I could repeat by heart."

Mary Baker Eddy

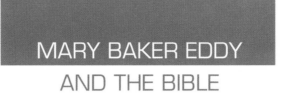

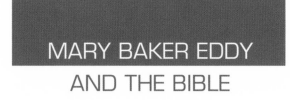
"Among the list of blessings infinite I count these dear...
the daily Bible reading and family prayer; my cradle hymn
and the Lord's Prayer, repeated at night...."

Mary Baker Eddy

"I became early a child of the Church, an eager
lover and student of vital Christianity."

Mary Baker Eddy

"[Mary Baker Eddy] once told me that even when a young girl,

she loved to help others gain an understanding of the Scriptures.

This gift for teaching was beautifully illustrated in the case of

the young chore boy employed by her father.

The little fellow could not read or write and knew nothing of the Scriptures.

Mary Baker taught him by reading aloud to him chapter after chapter from the Bible.

The boy was so inspired by this loving instruction and took such an eager interest in his lessons

that before long he was able to read and write.

From then on, every Sunday found him in his place in the old meeting house."

Irving C. Tomlinson

MARY BAKER EDDY
AND THE BIBLE

To Mary Baker Eddy the Bible was

her manna for the day;
her only authority;
her chart and compass;
the Book of Books;
her daily meat and drink;
her sole teacher;
her inspiration and revelation.

"The Bible contains the recipe for all healing."

Mary Baker Eddy

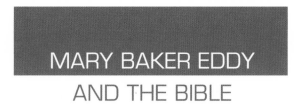
"The Bible is our sea-beaten rock. It guides the fishermen. It stands the storm. It engages the attention and enriches the being of all men."

Mary Baker Eddy

Sea of Galilee, Israel

"You will always find that what I have been thinking about and talking about has its counterpart in Scripture....The Bible and I are inseparable. It has always been so."

Mary Baker Eddy

When Jesus asked his disciples who they thought he was, Simon Peter answered:

> "...Thou art the Christ, the Son of the living God."

What was Jesus' response to Peter's reply?

> "...Blessed art thou, Simon Bar-jona: for flesh and blood hath not revealed it unto thee, but my Father which is in heaven. And I say also unto thee, That thou art Peter, and upon this rock [*petra*] I will build my church...."

The Gospel of Matthew

"...I have built Christian Science upon the Petra of the Scriptures."

Mary Baker Eddy

Model, Herod The Great Temple
Jerusalem, Israel

MARY BAKER EDDY
AND THE BIBLE

Original Edifice of The Mother Church

MARY BAKER EDDY
AND THE BIBLE

"...the Bible, especially the First Commandment of the Decalogue, and Ninety-first Psalm, the Sermon on the Mount, and St. John's Revelation, educated my thought many years, yea, all the way up to its preparation for and reception of the Science of Christianity."

Mary Baker Eddy

"The First Commandment is my favorite text. It demonstrates Christian Science."

Mary Baker Eddy

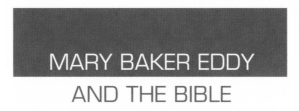

Can you find the answers to these questions?

- What precious book did Abigail Baker read to Mary?
  - How did this influence the little girl?

- What incident in Mary's childhood paralleled an experience that happened to the Bible character Samuel?

- How did Mary follow the Bible character Daniel's example of praying?

- What could Mary repeat by heart at the age of 12 years?

- List the childhood blessings Mrs. Eddy described in one of her published works.

- What did young Mary often choose to do instead of playing with other children?

- Which four biblical passages and/or books did Mrs. Eddy especially say prepared her thought before discovering Christian Science?

- What was Mrs. Eddy's favorite text? Why? How do we obey that in our lives?

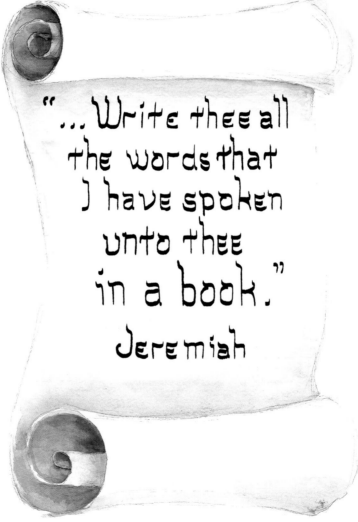

"... Write thee all the words that I have spoken unto thee in a book."

Jeremiah

MARY BAKER EDDY
AS AUTHOR

"When God called the author to proclaim His Gospel to this age, there came also the charge to plant and water His vineyard."

Mary Baker Eddy

"My first writings on Christian Science began with notes on the Scriptures. I consulted no other authors and read no other book but the Bible for about three years....It was not myself, but the divine power of Truth and Love, infinitely above me, which dictated 'Science and Health with Key to the Scriptures.'"

Mary Baker Eddy

"Heal the sick, raise the dead, cleanse the lepers, cast out demons."

This Bible verse in the Gospel of Matthew is written around the seal which appears on the Christian Science textbook.

"Before writing *Science and Health with Key to the Scriptures*
I had asked God for weeks to tell me what next I should do and
each day I opened the Bible for my answer, but did not receive
it. But when I grew to receiving it I opened again and the first
verse I looked at was in Isaiah 30:8."

Mary Baker Eddy

"Now go, write it before them in a table, and note it in a book,
that it may be for the time to come for ever and ever."

Isaiah

"Six weeks I waited on God to suggest a name for the book I had been writing. Its title, Science and Health, came to me in the silence of night, when the steadfast stars watched over the world, — when slumber had fled, — and I rose and recorded the hallowed suggestion....Six months thereafter Miss Dorcas Rawson of Lynn brought to me Wyclif's translation of the New Testament, and pointed out that identical phrase, 'Science and Health,' which is rendered in the Authorized Version 'knowledge of salvation.'"

Mary Baker Eddy

Attic room, Lynn, Massachusetts, where Mary Baker Glover finished writing *Science and Health*

"I had no time to borrow from Authors. Such a flood tide of truth was lifted upon me [—] at times it was overwhelming and I have drawn quick breath as my pen flew on, feeling as it were submerged in the transfiguration of spiritual ideas."

Mary Baker Eddy

"The works I have written on Christian Science contain absolute Truth, and my necessity was to tell it....I was a scribe under orders; and who can refrain from transcribing what God indites...?"

Mary Baker Eddy

When questioned by a child who observed her writing on one occasion, **"Mrs. Eddy replied with a smile that she was working on the life of God."**

Robert Peel

"I could not write these notes after sunset. All thoughts in the line of Scriptural interpretation would leave me until the rising of the sun."

Mary Baker Eddy

Sunrise over Sea of Galilee, Israel

"Christian Science is dawning upon a material age."

Mary Baker Eddy

MARY BAKER EDDY
AS AUTHOR

"It has always been my desire and expectation...
that my book should encourage more and more people to read the Bible."

Mary Baker Eddy

"With the reading of her textbook, 'Science and Health with Key to the Scriptures,'
Mrs. Eddy insisted that her students make, every day, a prayerful study of the Bible,
and obtain the spiritual understanding of its promises."

William B. Johnson

"And I saw another mighty angel come down from heaven....
And he had in his hand a little book open...."

Revelation

Referring to the above passage, Mrs. Eddy writes:

"This angel had in his hand 'a little book,'
open for all to read and understand.
Did this same book contain the revelation of
divine Science...?"

"Take divine Science.
Read this book
[*Science and Health with Key to the Scriptures*]
from beginning to end.
Study it, ponder it."

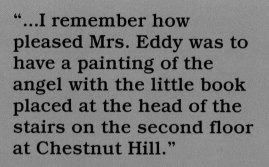

"...I remember how pleased Mrs. Eddy was to have a painting of the angel with the little book placed at the head of the stairs on the second floor at Chestnut Hill."

Irving C. Tomlinson

MAJOR REVISIONS OF *SCIENCE AND HEALTH WITH KEY TO THE SCRIPTURES*

First edition	1875	Lord's Prayer and the author's spiritual interpretation appeared.
Second edition	1878	Known as the "Ark edition" because the cover design had an illustration of an ark; printer's proofs filled with errors — only 167 pages could be used.
Third edition	1881	First two-volume edition; first to display the cross-and-crown seal; "scientific statement of being" appeared.
Sixth edition*	1883	"Key to the Scriptures" added but included only the "Glossary"; book still in two volumes.
16th edition	1886	Book appeared again in one volume; "Genesis," "Prayer and Atonement," and "The Apocalypse" added to "Key to the Scriptures"; index added and remained until the 226th edition when a concordance was made available in 1903.
50th edition	1891	Marginal headings introduced; "Prayer and Atonement" removed from "Key to the Scriptures" and made into two chapters; all but one of the literary quotes that headed the chapters were replaced with biblical quotes.
81st edition*	1894	Tenets of the Church of Christ, Scientist, first appeared.
226th edition	1902	Chapter "Fruitage" appeared; line numbering on the pages added; index dropped.
	1907	All testimonies in "Fruitage" except one were replaced with more current ones from those who had been healed by reading *Science and Health.*
	1910	"Animal Magnetism" chapter title changed to "Animal Magnetism Unmasked"; chapter title "Christian Science and Spiritualism" changed to "Christian Science *versus* Spiritualism."

*Note: Not considered a major revision.

Can you find the answers to these questions?

✎ What book did Mary Baker Eddy study before she began to write *Science and Health with Key to the Scriptures*?

✎ What Bible verse did Mrs. Eddy read and see as a directive from God to write the textbook of Christian Science?

✎ Can you recite the Bible verse Mrs. Eddy placed around the seal of the cross and crown?

✎ What does the word "indite" mean?

✎ Can you name some of the major revisions of *Science and Health* and describe what additions or deletions Mrs. Eddy made with each of them?

✎ What Bible verse appeared on the only wall hanging Mrs. Eddy had in the attic room of the Lynn, Massachusetts, house?

MARY BAKER EDDY
AS HEALER

"Verily, verily, I say unto you,
He that believeth on me, the works that I do shall he do also;
and greater works than these shall he do;
because I go unto my Father."

The Gospel of John

"'He that believeth on me, the works that I do shall he do,'
is a radical and unmistakable declaration
of the right and power of Christianity to heal...."

Mary Baker Eddy

"...Go and shew John....The blind receive their sight, and the lame walk, the lepers are cleansed, and the deaf hear, the dead are raised up...."

The Gospel of Matthew

Ruins of an ancient synagogue at Capernaum, Galilee, Israel (late second-early third century).
Jesus performed more healings in Capernaum than in any other place in Israel.

"I have physically restored sight to the blind, hearing to the deaf, speech to the dumb, and have made the lame walk."

Mary Baker Eddy

MARY BAKER EDDY
AS HEALER

In Anna B. White Baker's reminiscence is recorded a healing by Mrs. Eddy, who recounted the story to her household one day:

"Mrs. Eddy had told us of Miss E[aton], a young child of 12 yrs. whom she had healed of cataracts in her early work in Science — She was visiting the parents, and seeing the child in a very ugly attack of temper, sternly rebuked her saying, 'when you can see to do right you will see with your eyes'....The child instantly became still and her sight was restored."

MARY BAKER EDDY
AS HEALER

The following is an account of a mother who was accompanied by her two children on a visit to "Pleasant View" in Concord, New Hampshire, in 1897, to hear Mrs. Eddy speak. Her daughter (seven years old) had a pronounced, inflamed sore on her head.

"I wish I could make the world know what I saw when Mrs. Eddy looked at those children....I saw for the first time the real Mother-Love....This Love was everywhere, like the light, but it was divine, not mere human affection....I found myself weeping as I walked back and forth under the trees....I don't know how long it was until my boy came to me and said, 'Come, mother, they are going home.' I got into the carriage and drove back to the hotel, but that same conscious intelligence and Love were everywhere....When we got back to the hotel, there was no boil on my child's head. It was just as flat as the back of her hand."

MARY BAKER EDDY
AS HEALER

"Pleasant View" — home of Mary Baker Eddy, Concord, New Hampshire

MARY BAKER EDDY
AS HEALER

Irving C. Tomlinson recounts in his biography
a healing by Mrs. Eddy of a mentally
handicapped boy. Each day when Mrs. Eddy's carriage
would pass by the home, the mother told her child to go to the
fence so Mrs. Eddy could see him.
The son was healed.

"Now there is at Jerusalem by the sheep market a pool, which is called in the Hebrew tongue Bethesda, having five porches....And a certain man was there, which had an infirmity thirty and eight years. When Jesus saw him lie...he saith unto him, Wilt thou be made whole?
The impotent man answered him, Sir, I have no man, when the water is troubled, to put me into the pool: but while I am coming, another steppeth down before me. Jesus saith unto him, Rise, take up thy bed, and walk. And immediately the man was made whole...."

The Gospel of John

Model of the Pool of Bethesda
Jerusalem, Israel

In 1866 Mary Baker Patterson (later Eddy) healed a seven-year-old boy on Lynn Beach in Massachusetts of a deformity called "club-feet." Both feet were turned backward.

"At the time of the incident, the boy told his mother that...
[Mrs. Mary Patterson] was walking by, and seeing him stretched
upon the pillow with his feet covered....She put her hands under
his arms, and while he protested his inability to do so, told him to
stand, and when he was lifted to an upright position, she guided his
feet with her own, supporting him the while he took his first
feeble steps into freedom."

Margaret E. Harding

"...there came from [Jairus']
house certain which said,
Thy daughter is dead....As
soon as Jesus heard the
word that was spoken, he
saith...Be not afraid, only
believe....And he cometh
to the house of the ruler of
the synagogue....And he
took the damsel by the hand,
and said unto her, Talitha cumi...
Damsel, I say unto thee, arise.
And straightway the damsel
arose, and walked...."

The Gospel of Mark

Gustave Doré
"Jesus Raising Up the Daughter of Jairus"

"...when Mrs. Eddy lived on Columbus Avenue in Boston, she became fond of a neighbor's child, a little girl, who had never walked. Not seeing the child for several days, she called at her home....The child's mother, in great sorrow, replied that the child...had just died. Mrs. Eddy then asked to see the child and to be left alone with her....When left with the child...Mrs. Eddy took it in her arms and began to pray. Becoming conscious only of infinite Life, Truth, and Love, she became oblivious of the material situation until the child recalled her to human surroundings by sitting up and asking for her mother....when the mother came...the child ran to her, enabled to use her limbs as well as restored to life."

Clifford P. Smith

"Parents should teach their children at the earliest possible period the truths of health and holiness. Children are more tractable than adults, and learn more readily to love the simple verities that will make them happy and good. Jesus loved little children because of their freedom from wrong and their receptiveness of right. While age is halting between two opinions or battling with false beliefs, youth makes easy and rapid strides towards Truth."

Mary Baker Eddy

Healings of children by Jesus recorded in the Gospels:

Jairus' 12-year-old daughter raised to life (The Gospel of Mark)
Syrophenician's daughter healed (The Gospel of Mark)
Epileptic boy healed (The Gospel of Mark)
Nobleman's son healed at a distance (The Gospel of John)
Widow's son at Nain raised to life (The Gospel of Luke)
Multitudes healed (The Gospel of Matthew)
Multitudes fed (The Gospel of John)

Some healings of children by Mary Baker Eddy:

Infant with diseased eyes healed
A girl who could not speak healed
Baby healed of bowel disease
Granddaughter with crossed eyes healed
A 16-year-old girl healed of tuberculosis
Little boy who was crippled healed
Little boy healed of lameness
Little boy raised to life
Dead girl raised to life

Can you find the answers to these questions?

✐ Did Jesus tell us that we can also do the healing works he did?

✐ What is Mrs. Eddy's comment regarding Jesus' command to do his works?

✐ Can you think of similarities between the Gospel records and
   Mrs. Eddy's writings on the subject of healing?

✐ What were some of Jesus' healings of children?

✐ Can you name any of Mary Baker Eddy's healings of children?

✐ How many of your own healings can you tell about?

"The First
Church
of
Christ,
Scientist,
our prayer
in stone,
will be
the
prophecy
fulfilled,
the
monument
upreared,
of
Christian
Science."

Mary Baker Eddy

The first church built for Christian Science worship
(in 1886), Oconto, Wisconsin

"Were I to have charge of a church today,
I should have it founded on the Bible.
I should talk to them from the Bible.
I should direct their thought to the Bible,
and I should expect them to be obedient to
the Bible."

Mary Baker Eddy

"I, Mary Baker Eddy, ordain the BIBLE, and SCIENCE AND HEALTH WITH KEY TO THE SCRIPTURES, Pastor over The Mother Church, — The First Church of Christ, Scientist, in Boston, Mass., — and they will continue to preach for this Church and the world."

Mary Baker Eddy

"Whenever and wherever a church of Christian Science is established, its pastor is the Bible and my book."

Mary Baker Eddy

Interior of First Church of Christ, Scientist, Oconto, Wisconsin

"Your dual and impersonal pastor, the Bible, and 'Science and Health with Key to the Scriptures,' is with you; and the Life these give, the Truth they illustrate, the Love they demonstrate, is the great Shepherd that feedeth my flock, and leadeth them 'beside the still waters.'"

Mary Baker Eddy

"The precise day of Christ's birth, which remained in doubt for centuries, was also for long dated by many to 6 January.... St. John Chrysostom, a fourth-century Christian cleric...believed that 6 January would also be the date of Christ's Second Coming...."

Neil MacGregor

"[The Mother Church] was dedicated on January 6 [1895], anciently one of the many dates selected and observed in the East as the day of the birth and baptism of our master Metaphysician, Jesus of Nazareth."

Mary Baker Eddy

Original Edifice of The Mother Church

"...a church designed to commemorate the word and works of our Master, which should reinstate primitive Christianity and its lost element of healing."

Mary Baker Eddy

"...where is the house that ye build unto me?"

Isaiah

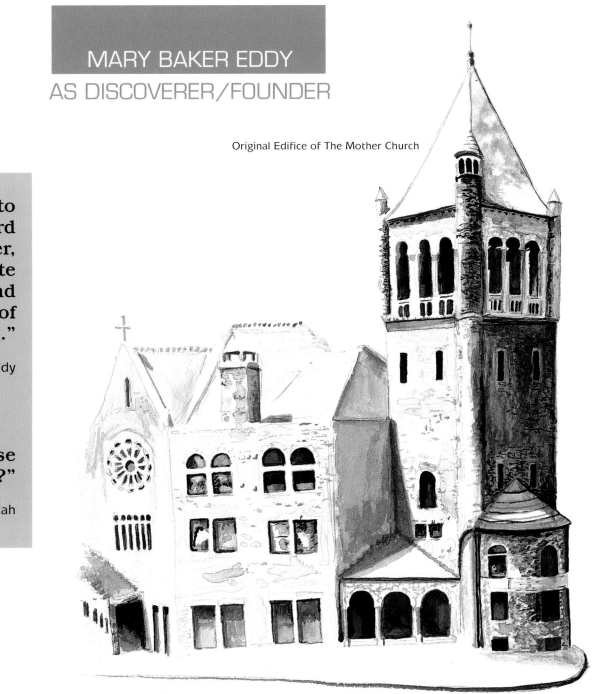

Bible scholars often refer to the burgeoning Christian community of Jerusalem in the first century as a "mother church," whose role was to oversee her many Gentile churches forming beyond the boundaries of Israel. One scholar has written:

**"The Church at Jerusalem, like a sun in the centre of its system,
had other churches, like so many planets, revolving around it.
It was strictly a mother and a ruling Church...."**

Benjamin Wills Newton

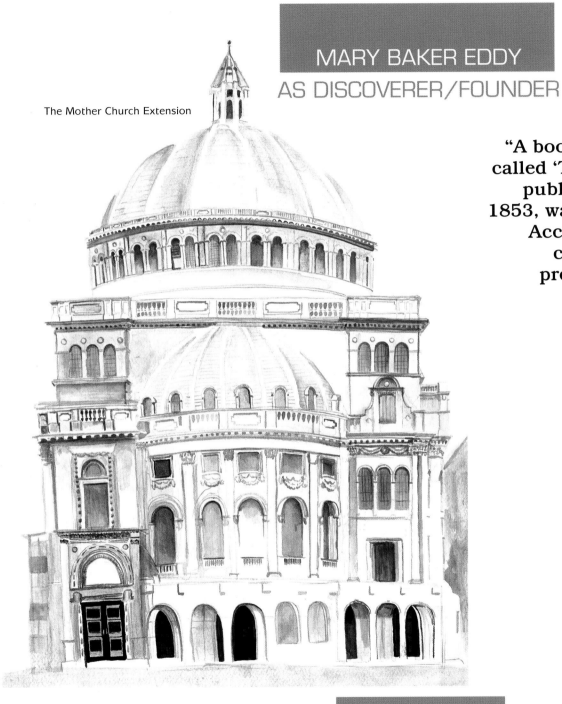
The Mother Church Extension

"A book by Benjamin Wills Newton, called 'Thoughts on the Apocalypse,' published in London, England, in 1853, was presented to me in 1903.... According to his description, the church of Jerusalem seems to prefigure The Mother Church of Christ, Scientist, in Boston."

Mary Baker Eddy

"...think of...the Mother Church,
— The First Church of Christ,
Scientist, in Boston, — the
Mother Vine, whose outspreading
branches cover the true disciples
everywhere!"

The Christian Science Journal, January 1895
(the year of the dedication of The Mother Church)

Olive branch

The olive tree is one of the most indestructible trees in the world. If it is cut down, new sprouts will begin to grow around the old trunk. It can bear fruit even with a hollow trunk. Some trees will grow to an age of 1,000 years or more.

Garden of Gethsemane, Mount of Olives, Jerusalem, Israel

"And [Jesus] ordained twelve, that they should be with him, and that he might send them forth to preach, And to have power to heal sicknesses, and to cast out devils: And Simon he surnamed Peter; And James the son of Zebedee, and John the brother of James...And Andrew, and Philip, and Bartholomew, and Matthew, and Thomas, and James the son of Alphaeus, and Thaddaeus, and Simon the Canaanite, And Judas Iscariot...."

The Gospel of Mark

"Christ and the 12 Apostles"
Early Christian fresco, late 3rd century, Catacomb of Ilaria, Rome, Italy

Scala/Art Resource

"...a letter was sent to twelve of [Mrs. Eddy's] most trusted students...
to meet together...to form a corporation to be known as
First Church of Christ, Scientist."

Robert Peel

The twelve First Members were:

Ira Knapp

Flavia Knapp

William B. Johnson

Stephen A. Chase

Captain Joseph Eastaman

Mary Eastaman

Ebenezer J. Foster Eddy

Mary W. Munroe

Janet Colman

Ellen Clarke

Eldora O. Gragg

Julia Bartlett

"As Mary Baker Eddy, I am the weakest of mortals,
but as the Discoverer and Founder of Christian Science,
I am the bone and sinew of the world."

Mary Baker Eddy

"No person can take the place of the author of Science and Health,
the Discoverer and Founder of Christian Science."

Mary Baker Eddy

MARY BAKER EDDY
AS DISCOVERER/FOUNDER

93

Can you find the answers to these questions?

What did Mary Baker Eddy discover? What did she found? What book has the rules for the Church?

Where was the first Christian Science church built to hold services? In what year was it built?

What did Mrs. Eddy designate as pastor for her Church?

When was the Original Edifice of The Mother Church completed? When was The Mother Church Extension completed? Why was The Mother Church founded?

What term did many Bible scholars use to describe the first-century Christian church in Jerusalem?

What term does Mrs. Eddy use when describing her Church in Boston?

How should Christian Scientists think of The Mother Church, according to an article from *The Christian Science Journal*?

How many disciples did Jesus ordain and what were their names?

How many First Members formed The First Church of Christ, Scientist, and what were their names?

In a statement to a pupil, Mrs. Eddy identifies herself as the "bone and sinew of the world." What does the word "sinew" mean?

MARY BAKER EDDY
AS LEADER

> "The true leader of a true cause is the unacknowledged servant of mankind."
>
> Mary Baker Eddy

"...I am the door of the sheep....
by me if any man enter in,
he shall be saved, and shall
go in and out, and find pasture."

The Gospel of John

"Feed My Sheep"

Shepherd, show me how to go
 O'er the hillside steep,
How to gather, how to sow, —
 How to feed Thy sheep;
I will listen for Thy voice,
 Lest my footsteps stray;
I will follow and rejoice
 All the rugged way.

Thou wilt bind the stubborn will,
 Wound the callous breast,
Make self-righteousness be still,
 Break earth's stupid rest.
Strangers on a barren shore,
 Lab'ring long and lone,
We would enter by the door,
 And thou know'st Thine own;

So, when day grows dark and cold,
 Tear or triumph harms,
Lead thy lambkins to the fold,
 Take them in Thine arms;
Feed the hungry, heal the heart,
 Till the morning's beam;
White as wool, ere they depart,
 Shepherd, wash them clean.

Mary Baker Eddy

"In April, 1883, I started the
Journal of Christian Science,
with a portion of the...Scripture
[II Corinthians 10:4-5] for its motto."

Mary Baker Eddy

"(For the weapons of our warfare
are not carnal, but mighty through
God to the pulling down of strong
holds;) Casting down imaginations,
and every high thing that exalteth
itself against the knowledge of God,
and bringing into captivity every
thought to the obedience of Christ."

II Corinthians

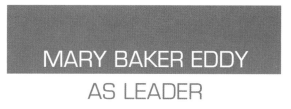
**"...*The Christian Science Journal* [was] designed
to put on record the divine Science of Truth...."**

Mary Baker Eddy

PUBLISHED MONTHLY · PRICE $2.00 PER ANNUM · SINGLE COPIES 20 CENTS

VOLUME 26   DECEMBER, 1908   NUMBER 9

THE
CHRISTIAN
SCIENCE
JOURNAL

FOUNDED APRIL, 1883, BY MARY BAKER G. EDDY
AUTHOR OF THE CHRISTIAN SCIENCE TEXT-BOOK
"SCIENCE AND HEALTH WITH KEY TO THE SCRIPTURES"

OFFICIAL ORGAN OF THE FIRST CHURCH OF CHRIST,
SCIENTIST, IN BOSTON · MASSACHUSETTS

**"Dear readers, our *Journal* is designed to bring health and happiness to all
households wherein it is permitted to enter, and to confer increased power
to be good and to do good."**

Mary Baker Eddy

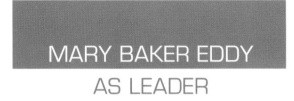
The Christian Science Weekly was first issued September 1, 1898. It was renamed *Christian Science Sentinel* in January 1899.

"...the second [Christian Science periodical] I entitled *Sentinel*, intended to hold guard over Truth, Life, and Love...."

Mary Baker Eddy

"...what I say unto you
I say unto all, Watch."

The Gospel of Mark

"...let us not sleep,
as do others;
but let us watch
and be sober."

I Thessalonians

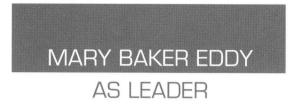

"...the next I named *Monitor*, to spread undivided the
Science that operates unspent. The object of the
Monitor is to injure no man, but to bless all mankind."

Mary Baker Eddy

The first issue of *The Christian Science Monitor* was published on November 25, 1908.

"When I established *The Christian Science Monitor*, I took
the greatest step forward since I gave *Science and Health* to the world."

Mary Baker Eddy

Bible verse appearing on each issue of the *Monitor*: "...first the blade, then the ear, then the full grain in the ear."

The Gospel of Mark

"The morning of November 25, the day on which the first *Monitor* was published, was dark and foggy, but Mrs. Eddy announced to the assembled members of her household: 'This, in truth, is the lightest of all days. This is the day when our daily paper goes forth to lighten mankind.'"

Mary Baker Eddy

Front page of the first issue of *The Christian Science Monitor*

In referring to the Bible Lessons, Mary Baker Eddy writes in her "Explanatory Note," read by the First Reader during the Sunday service, that these Lessons are "undivorced from truth, uncontaminated and unfettered by human hypotheses, and divinely authorized" (see *The Christian Science Quarterly*).

December 1889: "The Christian Science Bible Lessons" issued
(forerunner of *The Christian Science Quarterly*)
1898: Present plan of Bible Lesson subjects (a series of 26 presented twice a year along with "Thanksgiving") initiated in *The Christian Science Quarterly*

The following is a list, in order, of the subjects for the Bible Lessons:

- God
- Sacrament
- Life
- Truth
- Love
- Spirit
- Soul
- Mind
- Christ Jesus
- Man
- Substance
- Matter
- Reality
- Unreality
- Are Sin, Disease, and Death Real?
- Doctrine of Atonement
- Probation After Death
- Everlasting Punishment
- Adam and Fallen Man
- Mortals and Immortals
- Soul and Body
- Ancient and Modern Necromancy, *alias* Mesmerism and Hypnotism, Denounced
- God the Only Cause and Creator
- God the Preserver of Man
- Is the Universe, Including Man, Evolved by Atomic Force?
- Christian Science

"The Lord gave the word: great was the company of those that published it."

Psalms

"...I will give you pastors according to mine heart, which shall feed you with knowledge and understanding."

Jeremiah

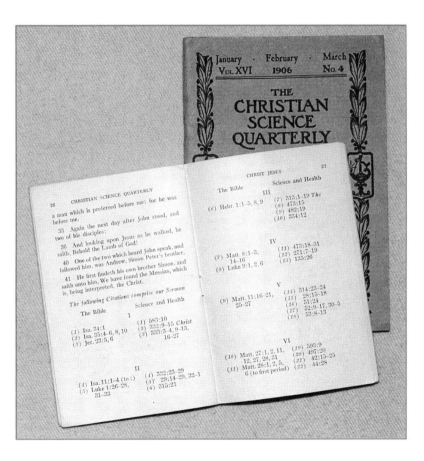

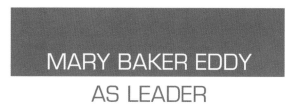
Can you find the answers to these questions?

Why is there no other way to learn about Christian Science except through Mrs. Eddy and her writings?

As Leader of the Christian Science movement, Mrs. Eddy founded periodicals.
What does the word "periodical" mean?

What is the name of the periodical that is published once a month? What is its purpose? In what year did it begin?

What is the name of the periodical that is published once a week? What is its purpose? In what year did it begin?

What is the name of the newspaper Mrs. Eddy started? What is its purpose? In what year did it begin?

What is the name of the periodical that is published every three months? What is its purpose?

When did the Bible Lessons start? What are the 26 subjects of the Lessons? What is their purpose?

"And Jesus, when he was baptized...saw the
Spirit of God descending like a dove...."

The Gospel of Matthew

"...he shall baptize you with the Holy Ghost, and with fire."

The Gospel of Matthew

"DOVE. A symbol of divine Science...."
"HOLY GHOST. Divine Science...."

Mary Baker Eddy

❖

"All the people need, in order to love and adopt Christian Science, is the true sense of its Founder. In proportion as they have it, will our Cause advance."

Mary Baker Eddy

❖

"My students need to search the Scriptures..."

"...and 'Science and Health with Key to the Scriptures'..."

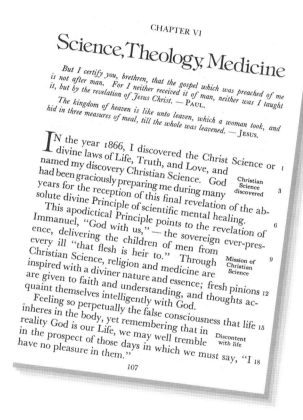

"...to understand my works, their motives, aims, and tendency."

Mary Baker Eddy

Some historical events (primarily in America) during Mary Baker's childhood and teen years (1821-1840):

1821 — Santa Fe Trail opens; Missouri entered the Union as 24th state.

1824 — John Quincy Adams elected President.

1825 — Erie Canal linking the Great Lakes with New York City completed.

1826 — First American railroad completed in Quincy, Massachusetts.

1828 — Andrew Jackson elected President; Noah Webster published *American Dictionary of the English Language.*

1829 — First steam-powered locomotive in America.

1830 — Church of Jesus Christ of Latter-Day Saints founded (Mormons).

1832 — New England Anti-Slavery Society founded.

1833 — Oberlin College opened (first co-ed college and first to admit blacks).

1836 — Massachusetts Supreme Court ruled that any slave brought within its borders by a master was free.

1837 — Martin Van Buren elected President; telegraph invented; panic of 1837 began, which caused bank failures.

1838 — Trail of Tears – Cherokee Indians began their trek to new land west of the Mississippi River.

1839 — Amistad slave ship was taken over by 53 slaves in a mutiny — John Q. Adams argued their right to be free; daguerreotype camera invented.

1840 — William Henry Harrison elected President.

Before the discovery of Christian Science in 1866:

1841 — John Tyler became President after the death of Harrison.

1843 — Beginning of large migration westward.

1844 — James K. Polk elected President; Samuel Morse demonstrated a telegraph, using a code of his invention.

1845 — Texas joined the Union as 28th state; potato famine in Ireland brought many immigrants to United States.

1846 — United States declared war on Mexico (ended in 1848); sewing machine invented.

1848 — First American women's rights convention in Seneca Falls, New York.

1849 — Zachary Taylor elected President; slave Harriet Tubman escaped to the North and began working with the Underground Railroad — 300 slaves escaped before Civil War.

1850 — Fugitive Slave Act provided for return of slaves brought to free states; National Women's Rights Convention in Worcester, Massachusetts.

1852 — Franklin Pierce elected President; Harriet Beecher Stowe's *Uncle Tom's Cabin* sold 1 million copies within the year.

1856 — James Buchanan elected President.

1857 — New Hampshire banned slavery.

1859 — Charles Darwin's *The Origin of Species* published.

1860 — Abraham Lincoln elected President; Seventh-Day Adventists founded; pasteurization invented.

1861 — Civil War began.

1862 — Lincoln's Emancipation Proclamation was published in newspapers in the North — freed slaves in Confederate states but not those in border states or recaptured territories.

1863 — Lincoln's Gettysburg Address; Louis Agassiz published *Methods of Study in Natural History.*

1864 — Lincoln reelected President.

1865 — Civil War ended; Lincoln shot and killed at Ford's Theater; Andrew Johnson became President; 13th Amendment abolished slavery.

After the discovery of Christian Science in 1866*:

"We welcome the increase of knowledge and the end of error, because even human invention must have its day, and we want that day to be succeeded by Christian Science, by divine reality."

Mary Baker Eddy

1866 — Trans-Atlantic telegraphic cable was completed — connected the Old World to the New.

1867 — Dynamite invented.

1868 — Ulysses S. Grant elected President; 14th Amendment — full citizenship to all born in United States except Native Americans.

1869 — Susan B. Anthony elected president of American Equal Rights Association; Elizabeth Cady Stanton elected president of National Women's Suffrage Association.

1870 — John D. Rockefeller founded Standard Oil Co.; Department of Justice created.

1871 — Charles Darwin's *The Descent of Man* published.

1872 — Grant reelected President; Jehovah's Witnesses founded.

1876 — Rutherford B. Hayes elected President; Alexander Graham Bell invented the telephone.

1877 — Thomas Edison patented the phonograph.

1879 — Thomas Edison invented functioning light bulb.

1880 — James Garfield elected President.

1881 — Garfield assassinated; Chester A. Arthur became President.

1884 — Grover Cleveland elected President; Samuel S. McClure founded first newspaper syndicate in United States; first long-distance service was established between Boston and New York.

1885 — Benz's automobile invented.

1886 — Statue of Liberty dedicated.

1888 — Benjamin Harrison elected President; George Eastman's camera invented.

1891 — Thomas Edison patented a motion picture camera.

1892 — Grover Cleveland elected again as President.

1893 — *McClure's Magazine*, New York, published "muckraking" articles from 1901-1912.

1895 — Sigmund Freud and Josef Breuer published *Studies in Hysteria*.

*Note the increase of inventions after 1866.

After the discovery of Christian Science in 1866:

1896 — William McKinley elected President.

1898 — Spanish-American War.

1899 — Tape recorder invented.

1900 — William McKinley reelected President; Sigmund Freud's *Interpretation of Dreams* published.

1901 — McKinley assassinated; Theodore Roosevelt sworn in as President.

1903 — Orville Wright flew 120 feet in 12 seconds in a machine heavier than air.

1904 — Theodore Roosevelt reelected President; radar invented.

1905 — Albert Einstein evolved the special theory of relativity.

1906 — Construction of Panama Canal began.

1908 — William Howard Taft elected President; Henry Ford introduced the Model T.

1909 — Sigmund Freud lectured in the United States.

1910 — First large suffrage parade held in New York City.

"Human belief has sought out many inventions, but not one of them can solve the problem of being without the divine Principle of divine Science."

Mary Baker Eddy

SOURCES FOR QUOTATIONS

p. 8   Mary Baker Eddy, *Retrospection and Introspection* (Boston: The First Church of Christ, Scientist, 1891, renewed 1920), p. 21.

p. 13   Mary Baker Eddy, *Science and Health with Key to the Scriptures* (Boston: The First Church of Christ, Scientist, 1875, renewed 1971), pp. 323-324, 582; I John 3:1 (*New Revised Standard Version*).

p. 15   Mary Baker Eddy, *Miscellaneous Writings, 1883-1896* (Boston: The First Church of Christ, Scientist, 1925), p. 110.

Mary Baker Eddy and Her Childhood

p. 17   Proverbs 22:6; Matthew 7:14.

p. 19   *Retrospection and Introspection*, pp. 5, 6.

p. 20   Jeremiah 1:5; Jewel Spangler Smaus, *Mary Baker Eddy: The Golden Days* (Boston: The Christian Science Publishing Society, 1966), pp. 17, 18.

p. 22   Sibyl Wilbur, *The Life of Mary Baker Eddy* (Boston: The Christian Science Publishing Society, 1907, renewed 1966), p. 11.

            Song of Solomon 8:5 (*The Bible: A New Translation*, James Moffatt).

p. 23   Robert Peel, *Mary Baker Eddy: The Years of Discovery* (New York: Holt, Rinehart, and Winston, 1966), p. 14.

pp. 24-25 Irving C. Tomlinson, *Twelve Years with Mary Baker Eddy* (Boston: The Christian Science Publishing Society, 1945), p. 14.

SOURCES FOR QUOTATIONS

Mary Baker Eddy and Her Childhood

p. 26   *Mary Baker Eddy: The Years of Discovery*, pp. 49-50.

p. 28   *Retrospection and Introspection*, pp. 13-15.

p. 29   Mary Baker Eddy, *The First Church of Christ, Scientist, and Miscellany* (Boston: The First Church of Christ, Scientist, 1941), p. 311.

p. 30   *Mary Baker Eddy: The Years of Discovery*, p. 15; Mary Baker Eddy, *Poetical Works* (Boston: Trustees under the Will of Mary Baker G. Eddy, 1936), pp. 32-33.

p. 31   *Retrospection and Introspection*, p. 31; Matthew 5:6.

Mary Baker Eddy and the Bible

p. 33   Psalms 119:105.

p. 34   *Mary Baker Eddy: The Golden Days*, p. 37.

pp. 36-37   *Twelve Years with Mary Baker Eddy*, 1945 edition, p. 16.

p. 38   I Samuel 3:4, 6, 8-10.

p. 39   *Retrospection and Introspection*, pp. 8-9.

p. 40   Daniel 6:10.

p. 41   Norman Beasley, *Mary Baker Eddy* (New York: Duell, Sloan and Pearce, 1963), p. 10.

SOURCES FOR QUOTATIONS

Mary Baker Eddy and the Bible

p. 42   *Twelve Years with Mary Baker Eddy*, 1945 edition, p. 16.

p. 44   Mary Baker Eddy, *Message to The Mother Church* (Boston: The First Church of Christ, Scientist, 1901, renewed 1929), pp. 31, 32.

p. 45   *Twelve Years with Mary Baker Eddy*, 1945 edition, p. 66.

p. 46   *We Knew Mary Baker Eddy*, second series (Boston: The Christian Science Publishing Society, 1950), p. 73.

Science and Health with Key to the Scriptures, p. 126.

Yvonne Caché von Fettweis and Robert Townsend Warneck, *Mary Baker Eddy: Christian Healer* (Boston: The Christian Science Publishing Society, 1998), p. 24.

Lyman Powell, *Mary Baker Eddy, A Life Size Portrait* (Boston: The Christian Science Publishing Society, 1950), p. 59.

Robert Peel, *Mary Baker Eddy: The Years of Authority* (New York: Holt, Rinehart and Winston, 1977), p. 114.

Science and Health with Key to the Scriptures, p. viii.

We Knew Mary Baker Eddy, second series, p. 73.

Science and Health with Key to the Scriptures, p. 406.

SOURCES FOR QUOTATIONS

Mary Baker Eddy and the Bible

p. 47 *Miscellany*, p. 295; Irving C. Tomlinson, *Twelve Years with Mary Baker Eddy*, amplified edition (Boston: The Christian Science Publishing Society, 1994), p. 105.

p. 48 Matthew 16:16-18; *Mary Baker Eddy: The Years of Authority*, p. 234.

p. 50 *Message to The Mother Church for 1901*, p. 32.

p. 51 *Science and Health with Key to the Scriptures*, p. 340.

Mary Baker Eddy as Author

p. 53 Jeremiah 30:2.

p. 54 *Science and Health with Key to the Scriptures*, p. xi.

Miscellany, p. 114.

p. 55 Matthew 10:8 (*Revised Standard Version*).

p. 56 *Mary Baker Eddy: Christian Healer*, p. 75; Isaiah 30:8.

p. 57 Mary Baker Eddy, *Message to The Mother Church* (Boston: The First Church of Christ, Scientist, 1902, renewed 1930), pp. 15, 16.

p. 58 *Mary Baker Eddy: The Years of Discovery*, p. 284.

Miscellaneous Writings, p. 311.

SOURCES FOR QUOTATIONS

Mary Baker Eddy as Author

p. 59   Robert Peel, *The Years of Trial* (New York: Holt, Rinehart and Winston, 1971), p. 279.

p. 60   *Miscellany*, p. 114; *Science and Health with Key to the Scriptures*, p. 546.

p. 61   William Dana Orcutt, *Mary Baker Eddy And Her Books* (Boston: The Christian Science Publishing Society, 1950), pp. 61-62; *Miscellany*, p. 48.

p. 62   Revelation 10:1, 2; *Science and Health with Key to the Scriptures*, p. 559.

p. 63   *Twelve Years with Mary Baker Eddy*, 1945 edition, p. 217.

Mary Baker Eddy as Healer

p. 67   John 14:12; *Miscellaneous Writings*, p. 193.

p. 68   Matthew 11:4-5; *Miscellany*, p. 105.

p. 69   *Mary Baker Eddy: Christian Healer*, p. 296.

p. 70   *Twelve Years with Mary Baker Eddy*, 1945 edition, pp. 61, 62.

p. 72   See *Twelve Years with Mary Baker Eddy*, amplified edition, p. 73.

p. 74   John 5:2, 5-9.

p. 75   *Mary Baker Eddy: Christian Healer*, pp. 44-45.

SOURCES FOR QUOTATIONS

Mary Baker Eddy as Healer

p. 76   Mark 5:35-36, 38, 41-42.

p. 77   Clifford P. Smith, *Historical Sketches* (Boston: The Christian Science Publishing Society, 1941), pp. 79-80.

p. 78   *Science and Health with Key to the Scriptures*, p. 236.

p. 79   Mark 5:22-43; 7:25-30; 9:14-29; John 4:46-54; Luke 7:11-16; Matthew 8:16-17; John 6:3-13; see *Mary Baker Eddy: Christian Healer*, pp. 22-23, 69, 79-80, 97, 167-168, 192, 228, 229, 232-233.

Mary Baker Eddy as Discoverer/Founder

p. 81   *Miscellaneous Writings*, p. 141.

p. 82   *Twelve Years with Mary Baker Eddy*, amplified edition, p. 156.

p. 83   Mary Baker Eddy, *Manual of The Mother Church* (Boston: Trustees under the Will of Mary Baker G. Eddy, 1936), p. 58; *Miscellaneous Writings*, p. 383; *Miscellaneous Writings*, p. 322.

p. 84   Neil MacGregor with Erika Langmuir, *Seeing Salvation: Images of Christ in Art* (New Haven: Yale University Press, 2000), p. 15.

    Mary Baker Eddy, *Pulpit and Press* (Boston: The First Church of Christ, Scientist, 1923), p. 20.

p. 85   *Manual of The Mother Church*, p. 17; Isaiah 66:1.

p. 86   Benjamin Wills Newton, *Thoughts on the Apocalypse*, third edition (London: C.M. Tucker, 1853), p. 33.

SOURCES FOR QUOTATIONS

Mary Baker Eddy as Discoverer/Founder

p. 87   *Miscellany*, p. 13.

p. 88   *The Christian Science Journal*, January 1895, p. 448.

p. 90   Mark 3:14-19.

p. 91   *Mary Baker Eddy: The Years of Authority*, pp. 31, 32.

p. 92   *Mary Baker Eddy: The Years of Authority*, p. 326.

           Retrospection and Introspection, p. 70.

Mary Baker Eddy as Leader

p. 95   *Miscellaneous Writings*, p. 266.

p. 96   John 10:7, 9.

p. 97   *Poetical Works*, p. 14.

p. 98   *Miscellaneous Writings*, p. 139; II Corinthians 10:4-5.

p. 99   *Miscellany*, p. 353; *Miscellaneous Writings*, p. 262.

p. 100   *Miscellany*, p. 353.

p. 101   Mark 13:37; I Thessalonians 5:6.

SOURCES FOR QUOTATIONS

Mary Baker Eddy as Leader

p. 102   *Miscellany*, p. 353.

Mary Baker Eddy: The Years of Authority, p. 311.

p. 103   Mark 4:28 (*Revised Standard Version*); *Mary Baker Eddy: The Years of Authority*, p. 312.

p. 104   Mary Baker Eddy, *The Christian Science Quarterly*, Explanatory Note.

p. 105   Psalms 68:11; Jeremiah 3:15.

❖

p. 107   Matthew 3:16, 11; *Science and Health with Key to the Scriptures*, pp. 584, 588.

p. 108   *We Knew Mary Baker Eddy*, first series (Boston: The Christian Science Publishing Society, 1943), p. 40.

p. 109   *Miscellaneous Writings*, p. 214.

p. 112   *Science and Health with Key to the Scriptures*, p. 95.

p. 113   *Science and Health with Key to the Scriptures*, p. 273.

ABOUT THE COMPILER

Kristy L. Christian. Kristy is a graduate of Principia College with a Bachelor of Arts in history/secondary education. She received her Master of Arts in religion with an emphasis on New Testament studies from Oklahoma City University. Kristy has traveled extensively in the lands of the Bible — Israel, Egypt, Jordan, Syria, Turkey, Greece, Italy — and has escorted tours to this area for many years. In 1997 she traveled as an assistant on a Harvard Alumni Association cruise through the Arabian and Red Seas, visiting Dubai, United Arab Emirates, Bahrain, Oman, Yemen, and Saudi Arabia. She is co-author of five books on *Teaching Bible History to Children of All Ages* and has published articles in *Scripture Forum*, a former publication from The Principia. Kristy offers workshops and talks on a variety of biblical subjects.

ABOUT THE ILLUSTRATOR

Robin Orbach Starke. Robin is a graduate of Skidmore College where she received a Bachelor of Science degree in studio art with a minor in art history. Her concentration while a student was in painting, drawing, and printmaking. Post-graduate work has included attendance at the Skowhegan School of Painting and Sculpture. Since 1989 she has been building and painting steel sculpture as her primary focus, although she continues her two-dimensional work as well. Her work is shown in several galleries, in public and private collections, and in museums throughout the United States. She has won several prestigious awards for her sculpture work and has participated in numerous individual and group exhibitions.